AF326781

SOON DONE WITH THE CROSSES
Poems

Poiema Poetry Series

Cascade Books
An Imprint of Wipf and Stock Publishers
199 W. 8th Ave., Suite 3
Eugene, OR 97401

www.wipfandstock.com

PAPERBACK ISBN: 978-1-6667-6557-1
HARDCOVER ISBN: 978-1-6667-6558-8
EBOOK ISBN: 978-1-6667-6559-5

Cataloguing-in-Publication data:

Names: Wilkinson, Claude.

Title: Soon done with the crosses : poems / Claude Wilkinson.

Description: Eugene, OR: Cascade Books, 2023 | Series: Poiema Poetry Series | Includes bibliographical references and index.

Identifiers: ISBN 978-1-6667-6557-1 (paperback) | ISBN 978-1-6667-6558-8 (hardcover) | ISBN 978-1-6667-6559-5 (ebook)

Subjects: LCSH: American poetry. | Poets, American. | American poetry—21st century.

Classification: PS3573 W55 2023 (print) | PS3573 (ebook)

Some of these poems originally appeared, sometimes in slightly different form, in *African American Review, Alabama Literary Review, Arkansas Review, Chronicles, Euphony, Manna, Modern Age, Poem, Poetry South, Southern Quarterly, Whiskey Island Magazine,* and *Writers on the River.*

We soon shall be done with the crosses
We soon shall be done with the troubles of the world.
    —"One of These Days"
        The Georgia Sea Island Singers

I've got a home in Glory Land that outshines the sun
Way beyond the Blue.
    —"Do Lord"
        Johnny Cash

Contents

CONTENTS

Birds That Alight on Faith

Help me also to believe in
the leanest saplings and twigs,
in something as flimsy
as a honeysuckle bloom,
as Theseus did, in my imagining, when
he tackled the Minotaur, or Icarus
when he flew momentarily
into the face of the sun.

Help in the way I've seen
pelicans and swans skim
mutely onto a lake,
thinking it solid as stone,
the way Saint Peter did
when he took his first steps
on stormy Gennesaret
before hearing the strife
cursing around his feet.

With only that thimbleful
of aerial surety, help me
to grasp those things
which never collapse
under the heft of this life.

The Parable of the Snail

My! You're a sticky wicket
        of examples of how I ought to be—

so patiently obedient in your quest,
        which seems simultaneously

endless and finite.
        But I could watch your constant,

nearly indiscernible pilgrimage
        for hours and likely never

learn a thing about loving
        my neighbor as myself,

nor whether you even give thanks
        from moment to moment

for every peckish blue jay
        who passes you up.

But by your humble, deliberate way,
        as you scale each mile of siding

toward the top of my tool shed,
        it's almost as if you believe

that it may be domed with other
        long-suffering, kindred shells

now on glittering paths of ease.

Blindfish

On my way through the Bs
in an old encyclopedia,
searching for some other gem
of obscurity that I've since
forgotten, I stumbled upon it,
also called *Amblyopsidae*, pictured
in stages of losing its organs of sight
in the onyx uncertainty
of Kentucky cave waters,
where the birth-brightness of eyes
must be like offenses of sin
till completely scaled over
and vanished into the translucent pink
of their body, from then on led
by a tense mercy of touch.

Lingering there for a moment,
I thought of the Apostle Paul's eyes
also being shackled with scales
after his Damascus conversion
before I noticed the recto
and under the topic of blindness,
three smiling children—
a small, bangs, lashes, and all,
talcum-white boy embracing
two darker little girls—
leaning to identify scents
of sunlit petals.

We're told that later
the children will study
Braille outlines of the flowers.

Glancing back at the fish
encircled in such utter black,
it seemed the poster child for faith,
and again, I thought about Paul,
before being healed, blinded
for a while to better carry
this gospel of these very children
who've truly learned to feel.

The Translation of Enoch

In retrospect, when I dreamt almost nightly
        of flying as a child, and of course,
without any referents of Apocrypha
        or Midrashim back then,

what I must have been hoping for was
        to so please God that he
would lift me till I, too, "was not."
        Now I have the illustration of Hoet

and the lithograph of Blake—visions of how
        it very well could have seemed.
Yet they, and even John Copley's *Ascension of Jesus*,
        though lovely in their serenity

and sentiment, don't feel right to me.
        My raptures happened
mostly during some state of unreadiness
        coupled with the bliss

and horror of being ripped from this life.
        Maybe Hoet's and Blake's Enoch
is to be presumed already seeing those gates
        of pearl, past that breathlessness

and vertigo I always suffered ascending. Maybe
        my diluvian dreams were merely
in the realm of swooning, thus why always when
        just about to break paradise's plane,

I shuddered and tumbled back to our fallen world.

Cock Robin, in Memoriam

February had been hard.
Even the doe who once
had three sweetly dotted children
was now down to
two winter-grizzled fawns.
And I had waited, and waited,
and waited on God.
On the morning
of the third day
of metallic ice and freezing pipes,
I found him
under my front window
in the one corner
without snow—
a dry vestry, if you will—
crumpled and colored
like an autumn leaf
till a few reddish breast
feathers fluttered by a breeze,
when his bill and crown
and tarsi were found,
and then the blind
but still bright eye,
though with no closure
of a tiny arrow
to suggest fowl play,
no resplendent shroud,
or cooing lamentations,
or lovely tolling bell,
or anything soothing
from the nursery rhyme—
only his chalky outline
of transfiguration.

The Diary of Perpetua

This much I found in common:
she and I both had visions or dreams
of victory over spirits of dragons,
presumably to attain the kingdom of God.

But our ecstasy and urgency
are where we part. In my conception
of eternity, I've mostly wanted
to return to this world as it looked
in the '50s and '60s on calendars
and in commercials, and to travel
America in a nice Chevrolet
from coast to coast, along the way
staying at picture-perfect Holiday Inns
with pristine swimming pools.

Mine has merely been a selfish heaven
of amber fields and gentle horses
endlessly grazing, and the still mirrors
of autumn ponds, and mild nights
of honeysuckle and whippoorwills

so far from halos of martyrdom
and ancient Carthage, and a hot,
jeering horde, and patiently waiting
in such good faith to be torn
asunder by marionettes of beasts,
then being finished with a sword.

Water Strider

Dirt roads puddled
after warm evening rain,
became a sort of

Mississippi Lourdes
quickened with the miracle of these
Jesus bugs

flaunting that
mustard seed faith, skittering
over their ochre universe

like small sepia stars
in time-lapse photography.
Though Gerridae

is the more
intellectual title, since when
have reason

and the less than
possible ever had anything
in common?

I mean, who
offers to feed thousands on
insufficient fish

and a couple
of bread rolls or decides
to catch up with

one's storm-tossed
boat by foot? Perhaps not
coincidentally,

in a kind of
cannibalistic Communion,
the bugs even take

of each other's bodies
for their earthly preservation.
As for their walking

on water, there are
those who will hold that the gift
is no more than their

evolution of balanced
design and millenary hairs on
such spindly legs,

while others surmise that
at least some chosen few are among us
who simply step and believe.

Birds That Cast Shadows Below

Camouflaged by altitude,
in the stern ecclesia of sunlight,
they are majestic floaters,
such momentary gypsies
that we fathom them
buzzard, or hawk,
or heron, or crow,
distorted as they sail

over strokes of Bermuda
and fescue, then on past us
muddling through ordinary lives,
to the bramble of some
dreamed, uncultivated room,
and there from a God's-eye view,
alight like the evidence
of things unseen.

Logos

Most days now the news
is not good, so I ask myself how
can scarlet and hyacinth macaws
still tolerate one another
on the same clay lick, and the same
of lakes bearing mayflies and loons?

How is it the stars and moon
yet sleep and wake together
in peace after these many millennia,
and why by now hasn't Saturn seceded
from its crowning glory of rings?

In the hot, blue August noon
and green, sinuated shade of pin oaks
is some of Heraclitus's strife and change,
the earth burning itself up in a phoenix-flame
to revive again from ash. I'm thinking
of Hopkins being torn between loves:
the cosmos of Duns Scotus and Ignatius Loyola,
"inscape" and "instress" more often at odds
than at rest, while another of my backyard's
little dramas unfolds as to how it all works.

From an abandoned armadillo hole,
a chipmunk peeps, quivers as if
hearing a hawk's famished skirl,
then scampers a few feet
toward groves heightened
with late summer light, but then
stops, quivers and darts back to his pit
over and over till I too bear the burden

of his life, feel the heart thump
under an ivory-plumed breast
perched somewhere atop
this deciduous world,
timing its quick descent.

The Fullness Thereof

With pollen's gold aftermath,
spring raising its weedy head,
come a parade of wood violets,
the deer with their sprightly fawns,
and judging by heavily leavened air,
at least a pair of skunks passing.

That poem of Lowell's has long
been one of my favorites,
where a skunk and her kits
are rifling through rubbish
for some smelly delicacy.

But this is more about amazement
in the season's voile clouds
haloed with silver moonlight,
questions of whether at the heart
of splendor, omniscience ever gets boring—
knowing every aardvark's quota of ants,
which zebra on each evening
will be seized in the lion's teeth.

And how can the heavens tune out
such racket of prayer from
all of earth's chirping birds?

Then too, it's strange to feel
blessed amid so much uncertainty
whirling about, in the paradox
of sometimes coveting even less
prescience, as one thinks of
with the skunks waddling off
thoroughly animal in a trail of rich

harlequin glory, side by side,
both buck and bitch,
to their own dark understory.

Carcass of a Vole

On a bus in Dublin, and fresh
from the Natural History Museum,
where I'd seen a silent zoo
of wolf and hippo, and even
presumptive skeletons of two
giant prehistoric stags,
I was mostly remembering
the intact, paper-sack cheeks
on a centuries-old hamster.

As I sat awaiting signs of my stop
for the Botanic Garden,
an elderly Irishman who
had lived in Saint Louis, asked
if I knew where I was going.
For a while, we chatted
of his family, his retirement,
and life back in the states.

After the gardens,
it had been suggested
that I visit the nearby cemetery
where more than a million
are buried. And after the gardens,
it was an irony of acreage
too onerous to contemplate—

those things that happen to who
you are during your hyphen
between birth and death,
the thought that in spite
of a decades-long
investment in life, you never
rose beyond dirt.

When I occasionally look
at a picture of my much-younger self
during a time that
most everything seemed before me,
the siege of creases
mapping my face weighs like
this muffled sparkle of autumn
in which, along with pooling
magenta leaves, is the small,
saber-toothed vole
who here succumbed
or was brought dead to my stoop.

Usually, I blame such gifts
on feral cats offering sacrifice
for sleeping atop my hood
and hunting the yard unbothered.
But why I let it lie there day after day,
studying it of evenings
as the tiny snout skinned
into grimace or grin—

I who couldn't pass
my mother's grave in winter
for years without thinking
she might be cold—
without understanding, left
it there nonetheless.

I'm almost certain
there were words
chiseled into a headstone
in Glasnevin—something put right
that must've felt like a cross lifted,
if only I could recall.

And yet in the perfect
opening for grace,
there's nothing but a timbre
of shadows, nothing
but waning light.

An Evening in Annus Mirabilis

So startled and pleased in the abundance
of bluebirds I'd seen this spring, especially
passing the rubbish heap on a hushed road
I love to drive just before sunset, that I refused
even to consider any toxic reason
for their brilliantly turquoise wings.

What looked to be a gold-bleached thrush
may have been only a glint on dappled leaves,
but not so of the largish, floppy umber rabbit
zigging past a stagnant pool impastoed
by algae, dazzled with tornadic gnats.

Each iridescent moment scanned
in strokes of damselflies, the fantasia
of tweeting hidden among elms
by this time approaches white noise.

A little later here and a familiar whitetail
would be out, both coon and possum would be
creeping through their twilight haunts,
and likely as not, the beige blade of an owl
slicing into the iniquity of night.

Maybe for one somewhere in Holland,
it's the yellow therapy of sunflowers
under a low, cumulus ceiling
like that of a Dutch master's sky.

But for now, beside such beauty as this,
piled with refuse of people's lives,
the landfill reminds me of Chaucer's Troilus
when he says sweetness couldn't be known
without knowing also about the bitter.

No wonder I marvel from craters
up mounds rising toward fearless clouds
drifting for what I imagine as empyrean places
of rest far beyond our current pestilence
and we who are pawns in the Olympian
game of asses and elephants.

In this brief peace, I can still give thanks
for the mild longing of doves, and for
the season's many fireflies—more than I've seen
since I was a child when they hung like berries

almost asking to be plucked from thick
Mississippi air, to sacrifice their angelic
lights for us to streak our dusky faces
in fluorescent glory as if come
with bright revelation for earth.

Birds That Crash into Glass

I would hate to think
it's suicide, that such
loveliness isn't eternal,
that a goldfinch
could tire of itself
or be so deceived
as to see a rival
in its own reflection.

What then could this
mean for the rest of our world?
That it must pass away
again, that there is never
utter satisfaction?

Some folklore says
the birds are spirits
moved to bring us
tidings of luck, omens
of death, or messages
from loved ones in heaven.

But what if it's because
they've begun to think
flying is overrated,
become fed up with leaves
not seeming green enough
and a moon being so dependable,
to think even paradise
could use some improving?

After James Dickey's "Cherrylog Road"

Here I'll use second person since
you were my Doris Holbrook of sorts,
not just because of your like first names—
though we were perhaps not so young
and not nearly so surreptitiously reckless—
but because it's you who for some reason
come to mind when thinking of the time
when I mostly longed to be "wreckage."

Back then, what place didn't seem
as secluded and clandestine as any car
graveyard with each new day thrumming
its own sweaty encomium of need?

Here I should probably make up
something about remembering one
particular evening and the special brightness
of a July moon and how an unexpected comet
sprayed across our ebon sky at the most
opportune moment, maybe allude to some
voyeuristic theme of crickets singing, and offer
a discreet metaphor of acerose air and the
starry penumbra of sweet gums mingling.

I'd be guessing, based on nothing really,
if I said you enjoyed listening to the surge
of the ocean or that your favorite color
was indigo. Here I could lie about almost
loving the mellifluousness of your voice,
lie about your voice being mellifluous.

I might be able to get away with comparing
ours to a few mythical romances, while nothing
so over-the-top as the strength of our infatuation
prodding us to poison, or one of us jumping
off the county's highest bridge into a rushing
body below when what was between us died.

Here, like in Dickey's poem where he's far
more enamored with the stories of rotting hulks
of automobiles than with his nearly anonymous
farm girl of the summer who doesn't speak or do
anything other than what he wills and then leaves,
like in that poem to which I return every so often,
alas, you also are being left forever by my
rusting memory speeding toward oblivion
up a never-ending highway of the past.

A Story of the Beautiful

"The story of the beautiful is already complete—"
—JAMES MCNEILL WHISTLER

On warm nights
when I've waited
for most other traffic to sleep
so I can drive the road called
College in peace, there is usually
a rather scruffy, bachelor pinto
just standing in the same corner
of a pasture lot, staring
into his own small channel of dark
except for the occasional cones
from passing headlamps.

Always the moonlight is as one
of Whistler's *Nocturnes*,
to my mind, an underpainting
of silver or gold shimmering
through our void.

If Brahms was right
and "a well of sorrow is love,"
maybe I keep traveling this route
because it's where I first
thought to myself, *I guess
I must've loved my father.*

And through whatever moths
and beetles mottling
my windshield, I remember
reading insects don't feel pain.

But of this horse, whom
I've no doubt personified,
I often wonder if he's basking
in such solitude, if the flint-fires
of lightning bugs and highest praise
of tree frogs are ever enough,
or is he there desperately watching
for some other, more
caring sign of existence
from one he looks to as lord.

Sea Horses

Always
last little trinkets
to be spooned
from their receptacles
of tempered water
into her aquarium, after
her palette of stones
and fancy guppies, so my mother
could watch the odd,
spiny posture
of zebras and dwarfs
for the grace of acclimation, appraising
each's anomaly,

maybe imagining a child's
widened eyes
as they gazed at the exalted colors
rising in spiraling columns—
a quivering "predawn dance"
of mating till, yes,
the stallions impossibly
give birth.

And there was the lore
of their bodies in China
being more valued than silver
because they were
thought cures
for impotence and wheezing.

Sometimes
there would be photos
of their mythological likeness
as in the sculpture
at the fountain in Trevi,
then some segue
from sea horses' genus
to Neptune's Hippocamp moon.

But none
of my remembrance
is about any
of this nor the cradle of lessons
on natural habitat,
nor the creatures staying anchored
within a few feet
of their mangrove.

My remembering
is to do with
not being a better son
while in quiet times between us,
as when I was trying
to equal her meticulousness
thinning the scarlet of cannas
and violet of hydrangeas,

or just before dusk
in summer when we sat
reverencing stardust sunlight
slant through thunderhead,
when hearing her soft hymns
that, no matter how
gorgeous with afterlife,
always sounded like tears,

how her memory
of relentless farm work
as a girl had brightened
to the release
of nostalgia, for my knowing
how things mostly were
between her and my father,
and never asking,
even toward the end,
how her life had been,

back from the age
when I was a boy, whether
indeed, her flowers
or songs,
our stabling
of sea horses
every so often
had ever
brought her
any earthly
joy.

Anathema

When a bronze starling
pecked her pregnant way
into the attic's
already rotting wood
and entrusted a trio
of blackish hatchlings
to one's presumed tolerance,
there was this uneasy privilege
of stewardship being
cast down again,
and for which there would be
no heavenly intervention.
Again, outcomes hinged
on samaritan goodness,
as they seemed to when
menageries made the yard
a meadow of burrows,
when a green turtle
wouldn't be dissuaded
from planting her young
just below the mower's swath.
Though this time,
with the starlings,
after too many mornings
and nights of their fledgling
flopping and squawking
over my attempts to do anything,
after a handyman was called
and told to get them out
first if he could but that
the breach had to be sealed,
the mother bird

soon returned aghast
at new boards and the tang
of fresh paint where
the crevice of her duty
usually was. There
she fluttered and hovered
as if cousin to hummingbird,
continually going
and coming back trying
to wake herself from her dream
till she considered
a near window's edge
of light, where for days on end
cursing everyone's rest
by all the gods she knew,
she tore, beak and claw,
through the screen
to bare glass
for that terrible stillness
she had finally sensed
in her nest.

Possum

Boo! peers the mime-white face
with slow ghost eyes—a loaf
spun in hoary, mussed tufts
of cotton-candy hair,
its chthonic tail singed to shame—

Deep South Anubis
summoned by moon-tide
from bloodlust for spiders
to copperheads to ticks,
perhaps to suckle the darlings
of its honeybee young—

still age-old myth
among Mississippi chicken coops
for prehensile roping
of roosting hens, then
as with Persephone,
dragging them down
to the underworld of appetite—

haint of persimmon trees
dropping rotting saffron fruit,
and of shallow graveyards,
or so it's been said, to end up,
all things ironically considered,
after some truck's heedless wham,

as nutrient in the rich sheen
of a raven's wings,
or just another aphesis
for those who bake of this body
with sweet red yams—

all the way through
its new genesis, playing dead,
quizzically, eternally grinning.

Listening to Nina Simone Sing "To Be Young, Gifted and Black"

Though neither of her chosen names
particularly black—the first supposedly
from a boyfriend named Chico,
and surname borrowed from
French actress Simone Signoret
seen in *Casque d'Or*
as a desirable mistress—

she, nevertheless, has the pedigree
of being born in Carolina
in 1933, denied this and that
until perhaps when she's photographed
wearing elegant white fur,
given an adoring bouquet
at Airport Schiphol in Amsterdam.

Still there is this gift
that she claims from the ghost
of Lorraine, this clear-eyed "dream"
of being something
in spite of everything else,
an affirmation for each dark girl
and boy's belief.

Yet the lyrics wrestle
her contralto into a prison
of generalities—the unquantified "million,"
an ambiguous "truth"—where no word
is nearly as vivid as images
of billy clubs and gestapo dogs' teeth,
nor any reason for "joy"
as beautifully blue as lupine,
or larkspur, or anemone.

Posed beside the Lyceum Marker Commemorating James Meredith's Enrollment at Ole Miss in 1962

Fifteen years after the burning cars,
and after acts of congress had chained
some of the spite, I too, entered
pro scientia et sapientia.
Now, this quarter century hence,
I'm back as a visiting scholar,
goaded to pleasantness for P.R. photos.

Who knows if it's just
the new breath of magnolias?
Still, I think of the tall, stunning
white girl who always glanced
whenever we passed each other on campus,
of our never waking on misty mornings
to share ripe figs and tea, of the life
we couldn't have had together then,
even in someplace like France or Greece.

Now here, as if a worthy paradox,
or perhaps to suggest benevolence,
an emerald-green sign tells
of this building being used as a hospital
for both Confederate and Union troops,

though nothing of one of the state's finest
in blue who pulled my father over
to ask him whether he thought
"that nigger Meredith was gonna
be able to stay." And yet,
remembering to keep my back
slightly arched and shoulders straight,
while maybe a bit glazed,
my smile seems graciously true.

London Rain

Other than for the dreary
rinsing making reflections
of colorful brollies pop up
like fanciful gardens, the world
seemed to have lost its mind.

Night lobbed brimstone
of Molotov cocktails
and rioting onto streets
over yet another black man
murdered by police.

But with morning, stories above
the to-and-fro, the splashing taxis,
and waiting museums,
having croissants and blood sausage
with a woman from Australia,

we each talk instead
of gladly leaving behind
our own homeland's
incessant summer heat,
of our excursions for the day—

mine through slow countryside,
breezes stuffed with muck
all the way to Stonehenge
for wonder, and for rest
among the calm fog of lithics.

Three Dogs in a Larder

after a painting by Frans Snyders

Were it not for this bounty
of gristle and bone, they could
dash like brothers on a hare's trail
or declare tug of war with any
old rag they found. But here,
each is part of a muscles taut,
muzzle baring, fiery axis of greed.

I give the two bigger, outside hounds
better chances of survival, or at least
to come away with meat, especially
the brute assuming dominion, reared
onto a butcher's block to snag
a bloody quarter of boar or venison.

The smallest of the three
that may be part spaniel,
snarls from behind the table's leg
at a hunkered, bristled black-and-tan
over choice morsels fallen to the floor
as if beatitudes on sharing, which each dog
clearly would rather die than accept.

Birds That Rebel against God

There are theories
that crocodile and canary
are essentially the same thing,
were not fearfully made, but
in fact, just one day emerged
from astronomical sluice;

that in a room stocked
with enough typewriters and paper,
after ages of swinging orgies
and bouts of flinging feces,
troops of whip-smart chimpanzees
would eventually hammer out *Hamlet*
or perhaps even best *Macbeth*.

And then there's archaeopteryx,
the dinosaur bird whose wings
were useless for flight but who
climbed to glide from one tree
to another, the ancestor
of Galápagos finches,
and ancient as hell—

some's sure-fire evidence
against intelligent design,
their proof of the link between
feathers and scales—a consolation
more believably amazing.

De la Cité de Dieu

> after a detail from a late 15th-century French manuscript
> translated from the Latin by Raoul de Presles

Though Eve's breasts
are less influential
than I would've imagined
and each figure is a bit
potbellied for perfection,
the pair seem comfortably naked.
Behind them is elaborate
masonry of a garden wall
crowned with a touch
of arabesque latticework.
Adam, as a bearded effete,
stands almost in ballet's
fourth position as if he
were subtly objecting
while spouse, on the sinister side,
modestly covers her crotch.
And in Aesculapian fashion,
spiraled around a sapling,
presumed the tree
of forbidden knowledge,
that serpent with coif and face
of a Renaissance angel
hissing his sweet persuasion.
Still yet without the Isaiahs
and Solomons of wisdom,
quetzals and lemurs
must have been screaming
in the moment remaining
of harmony before

the long kerfuffle begins,
the casting blame and talks
of annulment, before pangs
of labor and rebel offspring,
as all creation contemplates
this gloss of glory hoisted in
a woman's small, stylized hand.

Apokatastasis

From this theory
sometimes blamed on
Origen of Alexandria,
in true Hollywood fashion,
even the Devil himself
will finally be pardoned
for bruising the many
scions of Eve, perhaps
given the vivid wings
of a swan, or ibis,
or demoiselle crane as he
had ages ago and let slip.

Who knows? Maybe he'll
claim misquoting by Milton
or plead non compos mentis.

But according to this hash
of wholesale forgiving,
incorporeal holiness
has merely been wrapped
in "tunics of skin," and that
after the last judgment,
all will only be returning
to their unsullied form—
*restitutio omnium quae
locutus est Deus*, like
the sun and the moon
after eclipse.

Mural

Something about this love
in metropolis is miscegenation
between heaven and hell,

as for instance in one's pietà
of Jesus cradling the block's
lauded but unrepentant thug

under an atoning rainbow
and clouds of spirit pigeons,
where in such kingdom there's

no hierarchy among hookers,
drunks, prophets, and junkies,
and where killed children play

happily in gardens of purple
morning glories fertilized
with four-letter words.

Lete, an Eighteen–Year–Old Prostitute at the San Souxie Brothel in Juárez

after a photograph by Miguel Gandert

Her office is strictly utilitarian:
nothing on the monochrome walls
except one dark parallelogram
with a slightly lighter circle inside it—

no tactful icebreakers or delusions
of romance, just furnishings
for the moment in a sagging twin-size
shrouded with that satinet quilt
of hourly motels, the motley linoleum
floor a means of coming and leaving.

With legs crossed in cotillion fashion,
the way she leans back into bed
is reminiscent of Manet's *Olympia*,
though without courtesan adornments
of maidservant and flowers.

The hull of her body is smooth,
inviting, and her jaded face,
framed by dark tresses and bangs,
still surprisingly pretty even carrying
more than twice the time of her age.

It's almost inexplicable how quickly
her tinted, lifeless eyes could turn
desire into grief, but this is what I
remembered a good many years later,

when wrenching on my car, a flabby,
ponytailed, chuckling, grease monkey
dubbed Bubba, out of the blue brought up
how back in the '70s, down in Mexico,
he and some army buddies used to
get serviced by girls for a quarter.

**Listening to "Voodoo Child" While Imagining Sisyphus
Instructing Jimi Hendrix for His Eternal Labor**

Once from that sulfurous estuary,
      he's directed toward a wailing pyre

of material things to watch his
      custom Stratocaster burn and reverb

without antic magic or scores
      of screaming, mesmerized girls.

Now little more than a tumblebug
      and not one for another's self-pity,

always regretting his own accursed
      Corinthian spring that he bartered

for the secret of one of Zeus's liaisons,
      a silent Sisyphus points to Orpheus,

whose songs had filled even birds
      with envy, alone there mourning

just outside perdition's gates
      over his beloved Eurydice;

and then to Tantalus, who hasn't eaten in eons,
      standing famished and damp though

right below the crimson tragedy
      of ceaselessly shifting grapes;

to Persephone, who, for half of every year,
      from among the harmony of zinnias and roses,

must return as her fleshly self for Pluto's clammy leche;
          and to sallow Charon all day everyday

ferrying the dead, ferrying the dead, collecting
          each obolus, and ferrying the dead.

After this introduction to sorrows,
          he's probably told how things get worse,

that from time to time, he's likely to hear
          an echo of bongos or the strumming of sitars

as phantom pain of worldly longings.
          And when his futility is to begin, he's led next

to the base of a mountain where Sisyphus's
          rock and eternal rolling waited, then charged

to chop it down using only the edge of his hand.

Bluesman

Welcome to a world
      full of raunchy food metaphors
where nothing's more
      vital than jellyroll,
and life's marked
      by Gypsy predictions,
where so much depends
      on black cat bones
and mojo hands, in which
      familiars of choice are
crawling king snakes
      or buzzing honeybees who
sting all night long,
      often where mules kick
in other mules' stalls
      and then the only
answer that's right
      is the burning hell
of a .44-40 'cause
      a .38 Special most too light,
where it's easier to control
      the sun, the moon,
the stars, and the rain
      than one hardheaded
fine brown frame.

Blueswoman

A now frail figure
in sequined costume,
she stands on stage
in some run-down juke,
through the luxury
of bleach-white dentures
lisping sorry addictions
to low-down men
who love to roam,
narrowing our gulf
between us to no more
than the width of sharp lines
carved in the weary nest
of her face which
flinched sternly when
the song really hit home.

Scapegoat

Off hand, I can't think
of a more desolate scene
than William Holman Hunt's
shaggy image of sacrifice,
this lone precursor to Jesus—who
himself would hang pitiably serene
in so much of our sacred art—
crumbling, probably from hunger
and heat, into its destiny of sand.

Between its horns is such
outlandish beauty in a red braid
of flowers crowning the head
swirling with all Israel's fault.

Even if there's soft bleating
for the loss of lush pastures
and familiar shed, maybe
those dimmed eyes are at least
now mercifully unmindful
of the surrounding boneyard,
and are no longer frightened
nor spying behind, as goats can,
for Azazel's final assault.

Bonsai

Heavens,
the ingenuity of boredom—
in this case, dated back more
than a thousand years—

to Tang and *penjing,*   with cousin-words
in Mandarin, Wu, and Cantonese,
from scroll paintings and the *Noh* play

with fairy-tale rewards
for a selfless samurai
who burned as firewood
the adoration of his last little trees
to warm one he thought a traveling monk.
But for all the quiet distilled in its Zen,

all the beauty in its slant or cascade
or windswept styles,   the wonder left in it yet being
pomegranate, juniper, azalea, and bamboo,

there's also such bitter love of skilled starvation
and imprisoning the dream of its roots
from ever being among the mighty   unfurled by rivers of water,
a blessing of refuge to choiring birds and their daughters,

amid lacy doings of damselflies,
and embracing the light of the world.

Birds That Serve as Still Lifes

Indeed, the prerequisite is death,
and though the both of these
I'm recalling are common enough
crows, maybe found in a winter field,
then hung by the swarthy stems
of their legs, their scapulars
ruffled from Petrine crucifixion
and their satin primaries masterfully
splayed in Andrew Wyeth's
gouache and ink study, none,
neither pink-necked fruit dove
nor emerald-damasked cuckoo
has ever seemed too precious
a sacrifice for our lasting admiration
in one fashion or another, whether in
a milliner's abstraction of flight,
in Audubon's ironic conservancy,
or Daedalus's plan of escape.

Was it some avian part of the angel
which Jacob wrestled for,
something divine in birds that's
always been our deepest desire?

I've confessed my own early trespasses
of quelling the radiance of waxwings
and redstarts, along with all the many
others untitled and forgotten, not
for the exultation of making pictures
to be adored in museums, but
just to hold and behold lives
lived so much closer to heaven.

On the Aquarium in a Doctor's Waiting Room

There were those I recognized instantly,
        such as the bleeding heart tetra
and moonlight gourami. Some, I believe,
        are a golden type of glofish,

and a crew of bottom feeders which look
        like tiny carp never rousing
from their inclination, even if one of us
        in boredom disobediently taps the glass.

Supposedly, there are ways
        to tell if your fish are happy:
when they swim freely about the tank,
        when they rise quickly for feeding,

and when they don't hide in turrets
        of their ornamental castles or spend
hours on end cloaked among garlands
        of fluorescent wisteria.

Once I had a student become angry
        because everyone in class thought
her poem derivative of *Godot*,
        but as I recall, without the possibility

of anything Freudian, or Jungian, or any
        symbolism of faith, though her tree
was leafless, and there was this
        interminable waiting without action,

as is the case here where we
        are long forgotten except to be
called up for paperwork and copays, then
        returned to orange and amethyst peripheries

of always astonished eyes slipping
          back and forth through their clear,
uncomplicated place for what seems
          time immemorial till all of us are mostly

thinking of our world's beautiful distractions.

Torso of Pan

Impaled on a display staff
        are those muscular, acephalous shoulders
and twisting, fissured six-pack,

        though a copy or maybe even a copy of a copy
of the Greco-Roman original, and with
        only that slight wiggle of a truncated tail

to identify his deity. Even missing his strength
        of marble horns and the sorcery
blown from his panpipe, the gamboge patined lure

        of history still held me on the museum's stairwell.
It's amazing what comes back to you and when,
        as did the B movie that I must've seen at least

a hundred times in which its character
        of a lackey satyr pines always for unattainable
women, and that poem by Cummings returned

        about a menacing, goat-footed balloon man.
Likewise, almost a photogravure from
        my boyhood memories, is the stature

of Bill Robinson who showed up for paying gatherings
        at country stores to bite the heads off snakes—
rat snake, or blue racer, or whatever was

        your pleasure from his week's grab bag—
and whose secret anatomy
        was a whole other legend about which

some swore vows, so that I now see him silhouetted
        straddle in sunburst also having become a sort of
ancient of ancients, a pitifully weird Nehebkau with

        spells of writhing amulets harnessed round his wrists.

Rib Cage of a Deer

While a common enough occurrence along
such narrow, blind-spot roads,

this bleached vestige without head or hide, now
little more than corset stays—

probably polished for weeks by a coyote and some ravens,
nevertheless seems

somehow out of place as if something from Magritte
or Giorgio de Chirico.

Instead of its requisite kudzu tomb, I imagine it
as they might have:

lying amid an idle piazza or beheld through one's blue,
disembodied iris hovering

cloudlike over Bruges, with purple or yellow
or salmon salpiglossis

flowering into each negative space as symbol
of a surreal heart,

and twined around an also whitening sternum
the rife green

circuits of vine reviving dry bones
with everlasting life.

Shell of a Terrapin

A dusty, broken hull just outside the yard,
that may have been the yellow-bellied

or red-eared kind familiar
around these parts, its flesh long ago

pecked out by buzzard or crow,
is yet enough to say maybe it's right

that I don't forgive myself
for battering them into shards

in my youth, so that now
even words like *Terpsichore*,

even that Muse of dancing and singing,
can almost become a homophone of guilt.

But they were the enemy, the enmity
back then, Lucifers let loose among

forbidden fruit, our Eden of tomatoes.
Often, we would actually find them,

painted monoliths reared on hind quarters
to nibble each of the brightest globes.

I've since read that terrapins
aren't affectionate, are antisocial,

and will piss on you if picked up.
Still, and in spite of their filching,

it feels that they deserved better than
to be stoned like whores caught in the act,

as if we ourselves were without sin.

Roadkill

In the equitable light of Thoreau,
        as he mentioned more than once
                how the slain make provisions

for the living to gather
        at the welcome table, I try
                to fathom their excessive abundance

instead of just their mangled mass
        and venetian blood splattered
                like a Pollock painting, the whorl

of intestines pushed outside;
        snakes mashed beyond recognition
                into rattlehead copper moccasins;

the barn owl whose sole, ghostly wing
        beckons with gusts from each passing car,
                directing everyone's travel. I remember

Walden's order of untenable compassion
        and think of freshets clogged with frogs,
                which would be similar to the curse

on ancient Egypt, if not for accident.
        But it's still a kind of eclipse to witness
                the starching mink, a once quick vixen's glazed eyes,

or a kestrel's stricken plummet,
        still that same unnatural dark
                that followed when Macbeth

murdered Duncan, whose horses
		then went wild and began eating
				each other to signal something

awry, as do these many
		broken bodies dissolving
				into puddles of jewel-blue flies.

Hellbender

"Allegheny alligator,"
"devil dog," "mud devil,"
ugly "snot otter," "grampus,"
"leverian water newt,"
and finally settled upon
as "hellbender"—
able to contort
even the worst into
something worse—
how could we not loathe
your swarthy lore
and eerie feel?

And thought to be sent
by that old slickster
who tricks the foolish
into suicide by offering
them posted fruit,
though admittedly,
you live baptized
under the cleansing
of crystal streams,

where is there any other mark
of grace in your making,
some redeeming seal
of favor like that
of a cardinal's
dipped-in-the-blood cassock,
or as of congregant toads' all-night
trilling of joyful strettos,
or at least, as with
the enameled beetle's
whole armor of God?

Mule

Jack and mare made they
them both male and female,
a worthy lineage.
Among them are those
who packed the burdens
of soldiers through Sicily,
Britain, Afghanistan—once,
being so revered as to have
rhytons formed in their image.

Rows they've plowed
and Sunday surreys pulled
must number like grains of sand
by the sea, not to mention
all the mentions of them
from Herodotus to Aristotle
to us, and yet, still unnecessary
on Noah's ark of preservation
as they've nothing to love to beget.

Tennessee Walking Horse

Entering ribboned and wreathed,
       equus laureate with a gloss

brighter than lightning.
       What is more beautiful

than this monster of artifice,
       as spectacular and impractical

as nightingales and sparrows
       forced to sing backward or in Latin?

In the role of Poseidon,
       some mean little god

of machination bobs
       on the cloud of a canter,

then the flashy "big lick,"
       all the more exaggerated

by pain and applause,
       till nearly crouching

with cannons cradled
       so tautly beneath chest

that it's like watching a brother
       to Pegasus bound from soaring

under the cumber of lamed hooves,
       but still managing the craved cancan,

a gruesome goose step
        and rhythmic nod as inconceivable

as the circling question
        in his glassy eyes and urgent plod.

The Parable of the Crow

Eureka! squalls a crow from amid the mist
of our dense green summer after days of rain,
maybe for having found indisputable proof
of the origin of species that has lain there

for thousands of years now peeping through
an upturned leaf, or for glimpsing a mortise
and tenon which could only have come from
Noah's ark, or for discovering a thumb of salt

floating in a brook, and as old as Lot's wife,
having miraculously traveled from Sodom
to here, or for witnessing on the horizon
a new spectrum being born, or for mystic

intuiting that there's actually life on Mars,
or for finally having solved the riddle
of love, but most likely for having spotted yet
another wretch undone's patch of ripening corn.

The Parable of the Woodpecker

Who sicced you upon me
so early this morning,
God or the adversary of man,
in a somnolent state I asked

of the velvet-headed bird
ruining my fascia?

Knock, knock, knock!
came his reply.

Do you hear, I say who sent
your scarlet presence?

Knock, knock, knock!
rattled through the walls.

Why trouble such a sleepy,
but hardly Laodicean, who
isn't all bad and who at least
worries about being good?

Knock, knock, knock!
struck the epiphany

saying woodpeckers
just like pecking wood.

The Parable of the Cicada

We could protest we were
        not warned by thunderheads
                or the sky first splintering

into bright omens, that on occasion,
        we've quietened our own noise
                of fights we seem driven to extend.

We could complain that we
        already can barely hear
                the praise of wrens and tanagers

over jackhammers of commerce,
        that even the scarce woods
                and would-be quiet left to us

already hum nightly with babel
        of shrill though tolerable peepers,
                with songs of generally diurnal birds.

But then these fire-eyed emissaries
        of judgment could counter with
                their own penalties of creation,

with their cyclic jailing
        under the monotonous roots
                of incredible flowers in a blind,

damp abyss divided
        amongst worms and moles.
                They might say, *we've kept silent*

for seventeen years,
  for seventeen years you were free
   from the screech of our decibels.

You had seventeen years to get houses
  in order. Now gird up your loins while
   we come and shuck our darkling husks,

as we join in song and flight
  to share your treasured entitlements
   of sun and warmth and light.

Scherzando

A friend told me
        how his autistic son
                roundly ignores variations

of clouds and themes
        of emblazoned leaves,
                always searching the ground

for the perfect limb or twig
        as they shuffle through woods
                on their walks together—

not for any Dadaist assemblage
        in the manner of Rauschenberg—
                yet guided by an aesthetic of sticks,

perhaps by the curves
        of scaffolds or spurs,
                what would be his funny baton,

the maestro's own
        little joke for lightening
                whatever dark music

he may be hearing, just as what
        Mendelssohn and Monteverdi
                seemed to have sometimes had in mind.

Pale Green Victorian

In its heyday, a house set upon a hill,
which I recall being yellow trimmed with white.
There it seemed to me none would ever fall ill.

I remember the colors being so bright
because I always noticed when passing by
how they captured and held the breadth of sunlight,

especially from our spring and summer sky.
Turrets and shutters made it a fairy tale
castle where it felt impossible to die,

in whose yard you'd never find the words "for sale"
stabbed in grass near a blossoming citrus tree
nor spot a missing shingle or rusty nail

bleeding down the clapboards for others to see
and suspect something inside might be wrong too.
I imagined the owners blissful and free,

unlike myself or anyone that I knew.
After winter, it seemed their jonquils were first
to open, although this may not have been true.

Almost fifty years later, the thing that's worst
is the paint being dimmed from pastel to pallor,
the burden of being filled with unquenched thirst.

I'm not saying the house has gone to squalor,
but I never saw the roof clustered with leaves
nor even considered mold in the cellar.

Now there looks to be some damage to the eaves,
and the whole thing could be mortgaged to the hilt.
Still, it's not any of this per se that grieves

me more than the truth of Psalms on how we wilt
nearly as quickly as wildflowers in drought.
Childhood ponds become memories caked with silt

while promises of happiness peter out
like embers of what we once thought life could be
before finding ourselves on some fateful route

where we are left with the gall of fantasy.

Winged Victory of Samothrace

From Hellenism, it's merely another
        marble poem without head or arms,

and yet enthralling us since BC
        with her mysteries of purpose and damage—

some say commemorating the Battle
        of Salamis, but then others claim

the Battle of Actium, envisioned as
        alighting on the prow of a triumphant ship,

her chiton sea-rippled in descending,
        then after centuries being discovered again,

and further marred by speculation
        that the feathers of her folding wing

were neither bird nor Greek;
        that a vanished hand once held

an olive branch as Saint-Gaudens
        reimagined her, or perhaps a sword raised

for spoils as in Samuel Murray's version.
        Once she would be shuffled from the Louvre's

Daru perch and hidden for protection
        like a helpless baal outside Paris

at the Château de Valençay
        during World War II. When her extant

wing is finally matched, when later,
        after a partial hand and ring finger are found

and encased in glass beside her, she's bathed
        in x-rays for cleaning up and restoration,

as seems is so often done
        with the precious trophies of wars,

that they might stay carefully preserved,
        regardless of whether they're lost or won.

Before Being Deployed to the Middle East, a Group of Soldiers Eat Together at a Steakhouse in Grenada, Mississippi

Had there been
only thirteen of them,
the scene would have seemed
even more reminiscent
of Leonardo's *Last Supper*—
a few final moments
before sacrifice.

All their hands held
at Jesus's golden ratio,
though togged in camos
rather than robes,
and with no upper room
for privacy, they were indulged
beyond dry crusts and wine
sufficient for merely giving in;
theirs were the sumptuous
meats for contention.

If some were country boys,
no doubt, they fished
like Peter and Andrew.
Surely there's an outcast
of Levi proportions,
another bearing more
of a stigma than the rest,
and as likely as not,
one or two zealots.
In the probable background
is one's pushy mother who
wants for her son Boanerges glory.

As they have to finish,
it's not hard to imagine
any of them martyred
without immortelles to mark
his fall on foreign soil,
with precious few memories
at such a new age other than
for the requisite pass
at a tolerant waitress,
and perhaps this abiding night
of their discipling.

Birds That Sing in Winter

As odd as it seems, fluffed
against dropping degrees, from
power lines warming houses,

from icy fence wires, bunched
sparrows and chickadees claim
they have everything they need

in benevolent suet, sunflower seeds,
and in the all but invisible manna
they can excavate through snow.

Bright as they remain, some of them
softly singing like the titmouse
who saved Emerson one winter's day—

a sfumato of cobalt jays, alizarin
redbirds, finches' florin—each bird
steadfast on returning again soon

to the green box elder, cornucopias
of new fruit, and that dazzled mist
of cherry blossoms, as if recalling

a trusted promise saying none
of them could fall without notice
even in such wincing gloom.

Caesura

Amen, excepting
some wintry
melancholy or another,
for such drama
of gauzy gray clouds
and dianthus-pink sky,

across which, progress
easy arrows of geese
too lazy to have flown
further south than here,
honking now and then
for place in a poem,

and beneath this,
dusk symmetric with deer
over cold, fallow rows
of a cotton field,
rests like a good word
on the tongue.

Sugar Chile Robinson Plays Piano for Harry S. Truman at the White House

Before Duke and Dizzy
and Mahalia and Basie,
imagine the fates of nations
in such small hands,
on a cute as a button
rendition of "Caldonia."

Billed as "Frankie
Sugar Chile Robinson,
the seven-year-old Negro
piano-playing prodigy
from Detroit," picture
his elbowing and slapping out notes
as somehow easing the earth
after the first creed
of atomic Armageddon,
for moments, more important
than Germany or Japan.

Here after the death of FDR,
the bluesmen's champion,
sits this feared Missouri Democrat
in charge of everything,
between his two "bosses,"
Margaret and Bess, perhaps
dreaming of the quiet of roses,
maybe still preferring
his beloved Mozart
or a rondeau by Chopin,

but swaying now and then,
if only inside, when near
the song's mid-jump, about
a hardheaded, wanton woman
from across the wrong tracks,
the masses' little voice queries,
"How'm I doin', Mr. President?"

Postcard from Patmos

As we can surmise from certain accounts,
his exile wasn't so serene or immaculate
as Hieronymus Bosch, Hans Grien, even
Titian, and Poussin seemed to have believed.

Except for that affected halo circling John's
troubled head, Botticelli did a better job.
You'd think artists would be more attuned
to suffering. But of course, there were those

trees which greened and maybe some mauve
carnations which bloomed in spring, same
as anywhere else. Yes, there surely were days
when sky and cove became a correspondence

of blue, and always hills undulated to where
Petra looms, where we can imagine a break
being taken from those who were forced
to work in the mines coughing dark clots

from their lungs, from proofing scrolls
condemning subpar churches, and from
burden after burden of apocalyptic visions,
to write, "O dear God, wish you were here."

Feet Striking Zion

In my grandmother's final years,
        past the age of making spoon bread

and cleaning greens "through three waters,"
        before there were diagnoses for why

her mind had begun to fail, when
        most times all any of us got was a small,

toothless smile of recognition—or possibly
        of some other private joy—when her gaze

showed how little this world mattered,
        and when she could no longer walk

or speak in a discernible tongue,
        wheeled into one of her modest rooms,

day to day, she sat between
        an option of window or wallpaper

after the plaiting of her two long
        Indian braids of smoke-blue hair.

Off the mantelpiece, from an old
        Zenith radio flew her Jireh and Rapha

and Nissi angels of Brother Joe May,
        The Famous Ward Singers,

and especially Mahalia Jackson,
        summoning, "Move on up a little higher,"

proclaiming, "Soon as my feet strike Zion,"
        at which grandma would sometimes

momentarily return to us and shout,
        "Sang it, Haley!" all over the house.

Birds That Abide No Matter

Thank heaven, at least,
for the dreaming meadowlark
who wasn't told not to eat
anything after midnight,
who didn't go sleepless till dawn
fearing his hazel wings

being daubed with gel
for an ultrasound, nor the route
of a scope snaked down
the delicate flute of his throat,
who's not burdened for those
already with bad diagnoses,

but who rests among laurels
of proverbs and psalms,
expectant of being bathed again
in another rose-colored show
of providence when it comes,
how it comes, if it comes.

Dog on a Chain

Every day for years passing
the big, red shepherd-mix frame
there without shade tree,
head pats, belly rubs,
or anything else other than
a drab, cobbled home and his
small circumference of grass,

whether he was out in another
breathlessly pollen-filled spring
or staring blankly across
a new crown of hoarfrost,
I may have been thinking
of something like the mouthy
Papageno's lips being sealed
and him banished to a cave,
and so, I wished the dog freed
even if it meant him being dead.

He had given up barking
and straining against the links,
and now showed no interest
in the mocking liberty of squirrels
nor in sprinkles of mistflower
bluing beneath his feet.

Then after weeks of his absence
and his house being removed
for the obvious reason, I remembered
the rather sappy poem, "Rainbow Bridge,"
about a pet heaven, if you will,
where they play endlessly together,
and all feel loved and are healed.

Abishag's Task

1

How hard it probably was
to still see an old, some say,
syphilitic king as
the ruddy boy anointed,
as slayer of marauding bears
and blasphemous Philistine giants,
once the psalm on the tongues
of a nation of women
and with enough vigor
to be ravisher of Bathsheba,
yet always the apple
of the Almighty's eye,
now quaking from chills
even in Jerusalem summers.

2

The later, more carnal
of two paintings I've seen
comes to mind while thinking
of this girl concubine's
irreducible lot. Whereas the earlier,
fifteenth-century picture
is laughably genteel and Western,
the one called *David and Abishag*
by Pedro Américo, is uncomfortably
curious, maybe because
of their incompatible ages
as she lies losing her virgin warmth
unclothed beside him with only
a glimmer of memory rising

in his weak, careful eyes,
when she may have
so wished to be elsewhere
out in what could've been
many a Mediterranean night
under the language of palms,
being embraced by one
of her own choosing.

In Medias Res

So this is it, the middle, the center,
what's finally at the heart of the matter,
the transfigured hub, the crux come
at last after ages of anxiety ab ovo,
that equidistant point in one's circumference
of life, a so-called crisis state, when skies
can be as cornflower blue as Vermeer
would have loved, with evenings
of doves surely fond of one another,
when marigolds haven't lost their radiance,
plovers on the beach are still charming
to watch, and yet there's something about it all
that's not there any longer, or there's something
not now as it was expected to be, that's sought
in stored photographs, in ancient texts
of letters from father and mother about nothing
more concerning than an old neighbor
having died or too little rain for the garden,
without any warning of rogue hairs
and foggy thought, of the body becoming
oblivious to its former delights, but as if
by Homer himself, perhaps merely
meaning not to bore—so with no backstory
of Leda having been taken by Zeus or their
double-egg consequence of Castor and Pollux,
of Clytemnestra and the Helen scourged by beauty—
one is seemingly just plunked down
into some ongoing war of regrets.

Tribulation

Buffalo grass gonna come out tonight
as if by the light of the moon, and I late
with my herbicide again. Neither have I
yet tried filling with kerosene, as some advised,
an armadillo's trench beneath an old propane tank,
nor have I strewn a consensus recipe of moth balls
to rid the soil of moles. And what can really
be done about the little volcanoes of crawdads?
For the time being, those damnable ants
nudging their Babylon across what was to be
such a holy city, are both calling and priority.

At the garden center, I'm impatient, anxious
over myriad labels to study to find whether
I need granular or liquid, Borax or something else,
and whether it's for fire ants, or pharaohs, or carpenters,
learning words like *eusocial* that I feel I'll never need.
The store's lone other customer, who I'm sure
won't bother me, looks as though she might've
been a debutante some fifty years ago.

Vexed among poisons all claiming to be
the best, my guard must've seemed lowered
for a moment, the veil of my temple rent
just enough for her tremulous counsel.
Asking if I had found anything that worked,
she complained that she too bore enmity
for those terrible mounds rising
like adobe clouds with every soaking rain,
that they were killing her cherished bougainvillea,
which I believe she mentioned, she had only seen
one other similar to it somewhere in Venice or Spain.

About the armadillos, she'd had it, and determined
to shoot the next one to tunnel under her condenser,
but she agreed on the answer of moth balls
as a talisman against moles.
She quoted me a dollar amount paid
to get raccoons, then squirrels, removed,
but said she wouldn't be able to pay again
since her own and her husband's medicine
had become so expensive, since he was
now dying from two kinds of cancer.

The Garden

Checking a plump quince
and all the other dew-spangled fruit,
what was once given to be a joyful
tending without thorn or stress,
fell to my father and to his father
before him with obstinate clods
and ornery mules, with cutworms
and oftentimes parching droughts,
with hardy weeds and blazing delta heat.

What was meant to be merely
thumping cooled melons amid
the adoration of courteous animals,
somewhere along the inheritance,
became shooing brazen crows
and smashing thieving terrapins.

Though there was still the grace
of harvest, and yet, what was at most
to be an exalted body only moistened
in the mild, perfect firmament,
scarcely resembled my exhausted father
stumping behind a rusty middle-buster,
his clothes black as transgression from sweat.

Vigil

Brother to a cautious rabbit
　　　crouching under shadows
　　　　　and from moonlight's wings,

this, our being wake and about
　　　to a certain extent, is neither
　　　　　precious nor devotional. Rather it's

"just a few more weary days
　　　and then I'll fly away." It's "soon
　　　　　I will be done with the crosses"

since we are Hopper's *Nighthawks* here,
　　　snared in our own all-night café
　　　　　like the two men wearing business-blue

suits and gray fedoras who
　　　obviously don't know each other
　　　　　or care to for that matter, like

the auburn-haired woman in red who may
　　　be with the man she's next to, but nevertheless
　　　　　is so pale and loveless she looks almost dead,

with their jaunty but seemingly
　　　disinterested overseer in his uniform
　　　　　the white of dove feathers, who

for all their reticent weeping,
　　　offers only that shiny hope
　　　　　of sparkling-clean coffee dispensers

and a vow of continuous, fluorescent
        light even in these wee hours
                while the less troubled lie sleeping.

The Poiema Poetry Series

COLLECTIONS IN THIS SERIES INCLUDE:

Six Sundays Toward a Seventh by Sydney Lea
Epitaphs for the Journey by Paul Mariani
Within This Tree of Bones by Robert Siegel
Particular Scandals by Julie L. Moore
Gold by Barbara Crooker
A Word In My Mouth by Robert Cording
Say This Prayer into the Past by Paul Willis
Scape by Luci Shaw
Conspiracy of Light by D.S. Martin
Second Sky by Tania Runyan
Remembering Jesus by John Leax
What Cannot Be Fixed by Jill Pelaez Baumgaertner
Still Working It Out by Brad Davis
The Hatching of the Heart by Margo Swiss
Collage of Seoul by Jae Newman
Twisted Shapes of Light by William Jolliff
These Intricacies by David Harrity
Where the Sky Opens by Laurie Klein
True, False, None of the Above by Marjorie Maddox
The Turning Aside anthology edited by D.S. Martin
Falter by Marjorie Stelmach
Phases by Mischa Willett
Second Bloom by Anya Krugovoy Silver
Adam, Eve, & the Riders of the Apocalypse anthology edited by D.S. Martin
Your Twenty-First Century Prayer Life by Nathaniel Lee Hansen
Habitation of Wonder by Abigail Carroll
Ampersand by D.S. Martin
Full Worm Moon by Julie L. Moore
Ash & Embers by James A. Zoller

The Book of Kells by Barbara Crooker
Reaching Forever by Philip C. Kolin
The Book of Bearings by Diane Glancy
In a Strange Land anthology edited by D.S. Martin
What I Have I Offer With Two Hands by Jacob Stratman
Slender Warble by Susan Cowger
Madonna, Complex by Jen Stewart Fueston
No Reason by Jack Stewart
Abundance by Andrew Lansdown
Angelicus by D.S. Martin
Trespassing on the Mount of Olives by Brad Davis
The Angel of Absolute Zero by Marjorie Stelmach
Duress by Karen An-hwei Lee
Wolf Intervals by Graham Hillard
To Heaven's Rim anthology edited by Burl Horniachek
Cup My Days Like Water by Abigail Carroll